Dedication:
With love to Andrew and Aaron
who lived this and many adventures with me.

Acknowledgements:
Thanks to Connie Lounsbury
and Lucia Wilkes Smith, gifted readers.

For Alyssa
with every
blessing,
Delores Topliff

Whoosh
a true story

by Delores Topliff

Illustrated by Jessie Nilo

Whoosh

Printed in China.
First Edition

ISBN 978-0-9769031-1-6

Request for permission to make copies of any part of the work should be made to:

Verona Publishing, Inc.
P.O. Box 24071
Edina, Minnesota 55424

www.veronapublishing.com

Designed and illustrated by Jessie Nilo

Moose and deer, beaver and bear lived in the big north woods around our farm…

porcupines, rabbits,
squirrels, fish,
and lots of birds,
different ones
in every season…

But there were no owls in our valley.

Walking to school one day, I prayed for an owl to keep as a pet.

Dad said it would be better to ask God for a
fishing pole, a bike, or a new fishing reel.

Something easy for God to send, since
there were no owls here.

He said it might not
be God's will to
bring me an owl,
just because
a boy wanted one.

But I had told my school friends
what I prayed for, and they, too,
were expecting me to get an owl.

A few nights later, Mom asked me to run an errand to neighbors on the next farm.

It was dark and snowy cold.

I grumbled, but I went anyway.

As I climbed our hill,
I saw an unusual shape
on top of a bush
near our house.

The shape rose from the bush and flew towards me so low it brushed my head and parted my hair.

It crashed into our porch behind me
and flapped to the ground, stunned.

I picked up the soft shape
and ran inside shouting like
someone who has just seen God.

For in my hands I held
an owl.

Mom smiled and her eyes filled with happy tears.
She said my eyes were blazing like stars.

Before long the owl perched itself on my finger.
Its feathers were chocolate brown with dark markings
around his glowing gold eyes. He let me smooth his wings.

We placed him in a nice large rabbit cage and asked our friend, the Fish and Wildlife officer, what kinds of food owls need.

I fed my owl sardine pieces from a can.

I gave him water and milk from an eyedropper.

My little brother carried home a dead mouse for our owl.
He ate it fast.

My friends came to see my answered prayer.
Although there had never been owls in our valley before,
they had been sure one would come.

Mom gave us cookies and milk
while we tried to think of a name.

We named him "Whoosh" because that was
the sound his wings made when he flew fast,
"WHOOOOOOOOOOOOOSH!"

Whoosh could turn his head
almost completely around
when he looked at us.

It hurt my neck
when I tried to do that.

Every day my school friends came to watch Whoosh preen his feathers and sharpen his razor talons.

We all enjoyed Whoosh, but I was the only one who handled him. He could rip most things apart but didn't hurt me with his sharp beak or slashing talons.

After a week, his head began to droop.

"Mom," I asked, "do you think Whoosh is sad?
Is he sick? Do you think he'll be okay?"

She looked at me
and answered,

"Son, you love him and
give him great care, but
he probably misses his
family and friends.

He might be lonely
for woods and skies
and moonlit-silvered
treetops."

Our wildlife officer told me, "Whoosh might have been sick when you found him. Maybe that's why he came close to humans. Maybe now he could live free in the forest again."

I loved Whoosh.
But I wanted
him to be happy.

I decided to
set him free.

My school friends came one last time to say "goodbye."

Toward sunset, I asked my parents to walk with me to the end of our fields, where the woods began.

I held Whoosh in my hands, and asked God to help him. Then I lifted him up to the sky. And let him go.

Whoosh circled above us. Then he flew west towards purple hills.
Mom and Dad put their arms around me. I rubbed my eyes.
Mom said she could see me growing more into a man.

I'm thankful God listens to prayers and answers them.

I'm glad Whoosh came to live with us for a while. But I'm also happy he can fly free above the treetops in the blue daytime sky

or inky nighttime darkness.